BEST OF SCIENCE, VOLUME I, GRADE 2

TABLE OF CONTENTS

Introduction: Our world is changing at a furious pace. How will today's students keep up with this whirlwind of change? We must supply them with the tools necessary to excel in the future. These tools can be found in a sound science education that includes investigation and inquiry. Two guideposts to a good foundation in science are the National Science Education Standards and the Full Option Science System™ (FOSS) Standards. This book adheres to these standards.

Organization: This book serves as a handy companion to the regular science curriculum. It is divided into three units: Life Science, Earth Science, and Physical Science. Each unit contains seven lessons. Each four-page lesson contains a page of background information, a hands-on experiment, a page of math or language arts activities, and an activity that makes use of a graphic organizer. Each unit also contains a page of assessment and a page of science fair suggestions.

The Scientific Method: This book serves as a handy companion to the regular science curriculum. It is divided into three units: Life Science, Earth Science, and Physical Science. Each unit contains seven lessons. Each four-page lesson contains a page of background information, a hands-on experiment, a page of math or language arts activities, and an activity that makes use of a graphic organizer. Each unit also contains a page of assessment and a page of science fair suggestions.

Hands-On Experience: An understanding of science is best promoted by hands-on experience. This book provides a wide variety of activities for students to do. It is essential that students be given sufficient concrete examples of scientific concepts. Most of the hands-on activity pages can be completed with materials easily accessible to the students.

Science Fair: Students should be encouraged to participate in their school science fair. To help facilitate this, each unit in this book contains a page of science fair ideas and projects.

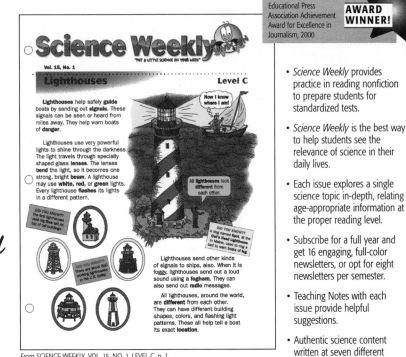

STANDARDS AND CURRICULUM CORRELATIONS

National Science Education Standards

Plan and conduct a simple investigation:
8, 12, 16, 20, 24, 28, 32, 38, 42, 46, 50, 54, 58, 62, 68, 72, 76, 80, 84, 86, 88, 92

Employ simple equipment and tools to gather data and extend the senses:
8, 12, 16, 20, 24, 32, 38, 42, 46, 50, 54, 58, 62, 68, 72, 76, 80, 84, 86, 88, 92

Use data to construct a reasonable explanation:
8, 12, 16, 24, 28, 32, 38, 42, 46, 50, 54, 58, 72, 76, 80, 84, 86

Communicate investigations and explanations:
8, 12, 16, 20, 32, 38, 42, 46, 48, 50, 51, 54, 60, 74, 90

Full Option Science System™ (FOSS) Standards

Earth Materials:
36, 37, 39, 40, 50, 54, 57, 59, 60, 61, 62, 63, 64, 66, 76

Air and Weather:
15, 16, 19, 36, 37, 38, 39, 40, 41, 42, 43, 44, 45, 46, 47, 48, 49, 50, 51, 53, 55, 56

Plants:
50, 51, 52, 53, 54, 75, 76, 78, 79, 80, 81, 82, 83, 84, 87

Solids and Liquids:
36, 37, 38, 39, 40, 46, 49, 50, 51, 52, 53, 54, 66, 67, 68, 73, 74, 86, 90, 92

Cross-Curriculum

Social Studies:
18, 39, 44, 48, 49, 51, 52, 53, 55, 58, 60, 75, 76, 78, 79, 81, 85, 91

Language Arts:
9, 13, 17, 18, 21, 28, 29, 33, 39, 43, 47, 51, 55, 56, 59, 63, 69, 73, 78, 81, 85, 88, 89, 93

Math:
14, 17, 21, 32, 33, 34, 43, 55, 69, 77, 80, 81, 82, 86, 89, 93

Health and Safety:
6, 7, 8, 10, 11, 13, 15, 16, 17, 19, 21, 23, 26, 27, 31, 32, 33, 34, 44, 45, 49, 51, 52, 53, 55, 58, 59, 82, 83

Art:
30, 39, 42, 44, 47, 48, 51, 58, 60, 62, 63, 64, 69, 70, 78, 81, 82, 90, 92, 93, 94

OVERALL ASSESSMENT

🔍 **Directions:** Darken the circle by the answer that correctly completes each statement.

1. People have five senses: sight, touch, taste, hearing, and _____.
- Ⓐ memory
- Ⓑ sleep
- Ⓒ smell

2. The sense of touch allows you to feel temperature, pressure, and _____.
- Ⓐ happy
- Ⓑ smells
- Ⓒ pain

3. Clouds are made of tiny drops of _____.
- Ⓐ weather
- Ⓑ water
- Ⓒ dirt

4. A _____ is a storm that has a funnel shape.
- Ⓐ hurricane
- Ⓑ volcano
- Ⓒ tornado

5. The Earth is made up of _____ layers.
- Ⓐ two
- Ⓑ three
- Ⓒ seven

6. _____ of corn grow on a stalk.
- Ⓐ Ears
- Ⓑ Eyes
- Ⓒ Hands

7. Too much sugar can cause tooth _____.
- Ⓐ paste
- Ⓑ decay
- Ⓒ candy

8. _____ is made from the beans of the cacao tree.
- Ⓐ Chocolate
- Ⓑ Cow milk
- Ⓒ Ink

UNIT 1 ASSESSMENT

🔍 **Directions:** Darken the circle by the answer that correctly completes each statement.

1. Our _____ help us with our sense of touch.
Ⓐ fingers
Ⓑ eyes
Ⓒ ears

2. The _____ is the colored part of the eye.
Ⓐ iris
Ⓑ lens
Ⓒ pupil

3. The _____ is the body part that gets messages from all of the senses.
Ⓐ heart
Ⓑ nose
Ⓒ brain

4. People must have _____ to see.
Ⓐ glasses
Ⓑ light
Ⓒ ears

5. The _____ vibrates and sends messages about sounds to the brain.
Ⓐ eardrum
Ⓑ eye
Ⓒ foot

6. The senses of taste and _____ work together to help us enjoy the taste of food.
Ⓐ touch
Ⓑ smell
Ⓒ hearing

7. Your heart beats more slowly when you _____.
Ⓐ run
Ⓑ dance
Ⓒ sleep

8. Your _____ helps you to remember things.
Ⓐ eye
Ⓑ heart
Ⓒ memory

UNIT 1 SCIENCE FAIR IDEAS

The science fair is coming! You can learn more about the world you live in. What would you like to learn about? Use the scientific method. Follow these steps.

1. Problem: How does the eye work?

2. Hypothesis: A model of the eye can help show how the eye works.

3. Experimentation: Make a scale model. Materials: Styrofoam ball or clay, plastic knife, art supplies.

4. Observation: A model of the eye shows all the parts. This helps to explain how all the parts work together to give sight.

5. Conclusion: A model is a hands-on way to learn how the eye works.

6. Comparison: The conclusion and hypothesis agree.

7. Presentation: Label all the parts of the eye on the model. Prepare a report to explain your results. Show your model and report.

8. Resources: Tell the books you used. Tell who helped you get materials and set up the experiment.

Other Project Ideas ~~~~~~~~~~~~~~~~~~~~~~~~~~~~~~

1. Make a model of an ear or nose.

2. What happens if people do not get enough sleep?

3. How do your senses help you to learn about things around you?

YOUR SENSES

Think about your five senses. You have the senses of sight, hearing, taste, touch, and smell. Your senses give you **information** about everything around you. This information is called **sensory input**.

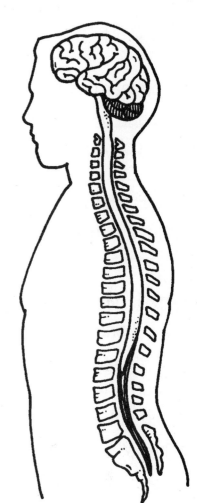

Your brain **receives** the sensory input. Then, it helps you to decide what to do. Your brain may tell you to **react** to the information. Your reaction is called **sensory output**. Have you ever covered your ears when you heard a loud noise? Have you ever put on a jacket when you felt cold? These are kinds of sensory output.

Stress is a special kind of sensory input. Stress can be good or bad. Your brain helps your body to react to stress. It tells you to smile when you are happy. Your brain also tells you to move your hand if you touch something hot.

YOUR SENSES, P. 2
LAB TIME

You learn many things with your sense of touch. You can tell if things are rough or smooth. You can tell their shape. You can also feel if they are hot or cold. How does your sense of touch work? Let's find out.

> **You will need:** 3 cups; hot, cold, and warm water; clock with second hand

Step 1: You will need an adult to help you. Fill one cup with cold water. Fill another cup with warm water. Fill the last cup with hot water. The hot water should not be too hot. You do not want to burn yourself.

Step 2: Put your left hand in the hot water. Put your right hand in the cold water. Keep your hands in the water for one minute.

Step 3: Then, put both hands in the warm water.

How does your right hand feel in the warm water? How does your left hand feel in the warm water? What does this tell you about how we feel?

YOUR SENSES, P. 3
PUT ON YOUR THINKING CAP

✏️ Writing About Science

Every day you observe things. You use your senses to learn about the world. Read the sentence beginnings below. Use your senses to complete each sentence.

This morning, I tasted _____.

On my way to school, I saw _____.

In school, I heard _____.

After school, I smelled _____.

At bedtime, I felt _____.

Thinking About Things

Stress is a special kind of sensory input. Stress can be good or bad. Think about things you have seen in the last two days. Did you see something that made you happy? Did you see something that made you sad? What did you do or say? How did your body react when you saw these things? Get another piece of paper. Write a few sentences that tell your feelings about what you saw.

YOUR SENSES, P. 4
FIGURE IT OUT!

We learn about the world by using our senses. Our senses are seeing, hearing, smelling, tasting, and touching.

🔍 **Directions:** How do we learn these things? Draw lines to show.

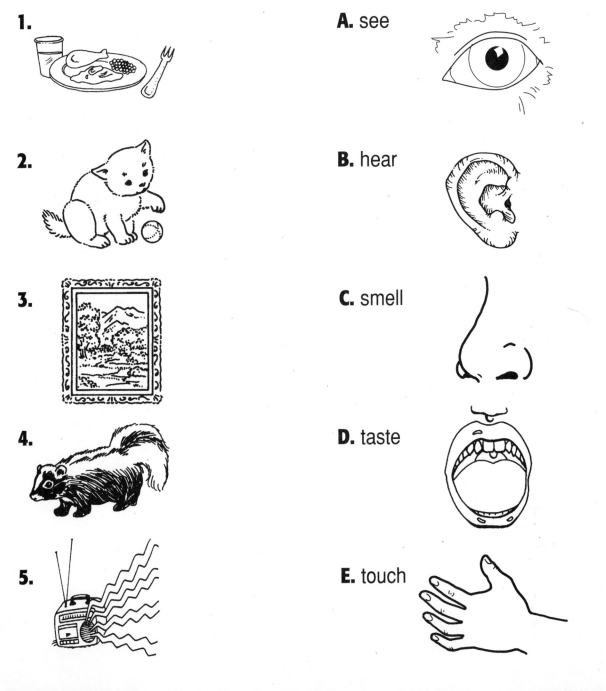

1.

A. see

2.

B. hear

3.

C. smell

4.

D. taste

5.

E. touch

YOUR EYES

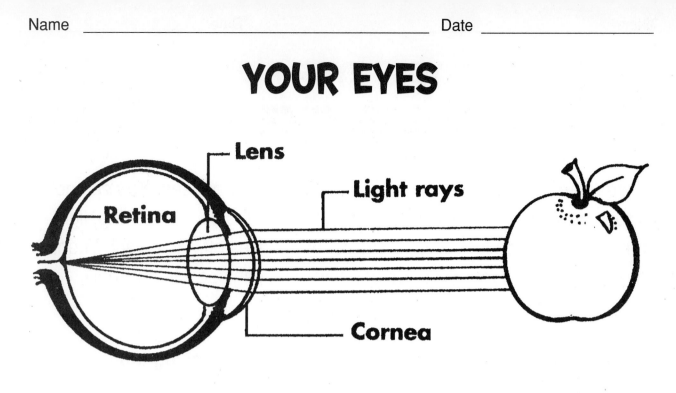

Do you like to read books or paint pictures? Do you like to watch TV or play video games? What things are in your classroom? How can you tell?

The sense we use most is sight. When you look at things, you use two important parts of your body, your eyes. Your eyes help you to see. They send messages to your brain about things you see.

The **iris** is the colored part of the eye. It controls the amount of light that enters the eye. The **pupil** is the opening in the iris. The **lens** is inside the eye. Light passes through the pupil of the eye. The lens bends the light. Then, the light lands on the **retina**.

The retina has special parts called **rods** and **cones**. When light hits the retina, the rods and cones gather information. They send the information to the brain. This information tells the brain what the eye is seeing.

YOUR EYES, P. 2
LAB TIME

You need light to see. If there is no light, you cannot see. You can get around without seeing. But it is not easy. For you to see something, light must be shining on it. The light reflects, or bounces off, the object. Then, the light travels to your eyes. Do you think you can see without light? Let's find out.

You will need: shoe box, crayon, scissors, masking tape, black construction paper

---

Step 1: Use the scissors to cut a 1-inch hole in one end of the shoe box. Ask an adult for help if you need it.

Step 2: Tape a crayon inside the other end of the box. Put the lid on the box.

Step 3: Roll up the black paper so it will fit in the hole.

Step 4: Look through the rolled paper into the box. What do you see?

Step 5: Lift the lid of the box a little. Now, what do you see?

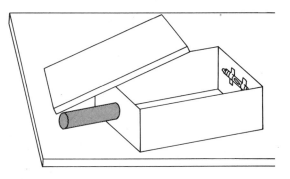

What did you see when the lid was closed? What did you see when the lid was lifted? Why couldn't you see the crayon in the dark?

YOUR EYES, P. 3
PUT ON YOUR THINKING CAP

Science Words

🔍 **Directions:** Draw a line to match each word to its definition.

1. lens

a. the colored part of the eye

2. retina

b. the part of the eye that bends the light

3. iris

c. the opening in the iris

4. pupil

d. the back part of the eye

✏️ Writing About Science

Look at the picture for 20 seconds. Then, cover the picture. On another piece of paper, write down everything you remember seeing.

YOUR EYES, P. 4
FIGURE IT OUT!

Eye Tricks

Sometimes your eyes can trick you. One trick is called an **optical illusion**. Things are not the way they appear. Look at the two lines below. Which line is longer?

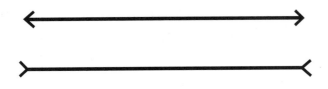

Use a ruler to measure the two lines. Do not measure the pointed ends. Which line is longer?

Look at the two black circles. Which black circle is bigger?

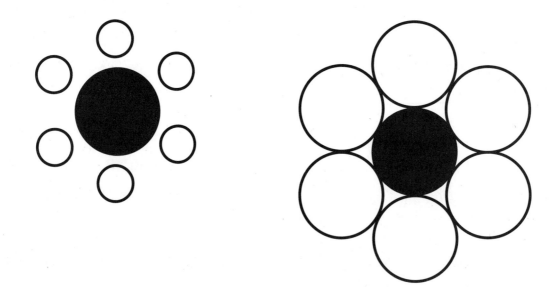

Can you think of any other optical illusions?

YOUR EARS

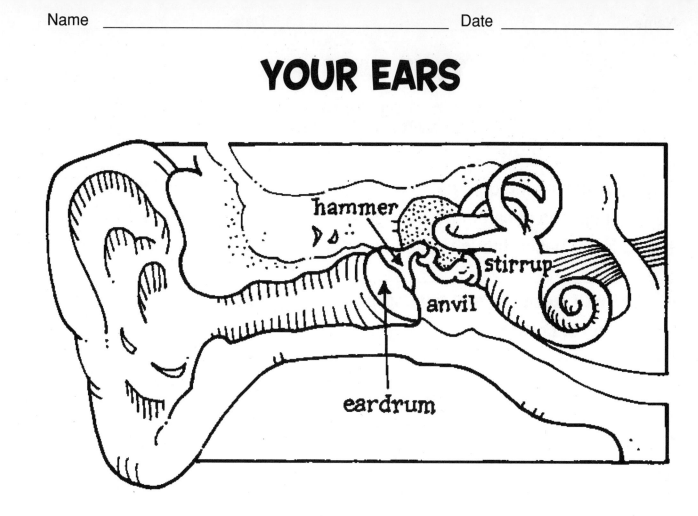

Your ears help you to hear. Sound is made of moving air, or **vibrations**. Your ear catches the sound vibrations. Then, they hit a circle of skin called the **eardrum**. The eardrum begins to vibrate, or shake. This makes tiny parts in your **inner ear** shake. These parts send a message to the brain. Now, you can hear!

Sometimes, ears don't work. They can be hurt by illness or medicine. They can be harmed by too much loud noise. Some people are born not able to hear. People who can hear only a little are **hearing-impaired**. People who cannot hear at all are **deaf**.

People who cannot hear must learn new ways to **communicate**. They may learn to "read" lips. They can tell what people are saying by watching their lips move. They may also learn to use hand signs. They may have special devices to help them to use the telephone or TV.

YOUR EARS, P. 2
LAB TIME

Sound moves through the air to your ears. Sound can travel through other things, too. It can move through water, air, and the ground. Does sound travel better through cotton or air? Let's find out.

You will need: 2 self-sealing plastic bags, an alarm clock that ticks, cotton

---

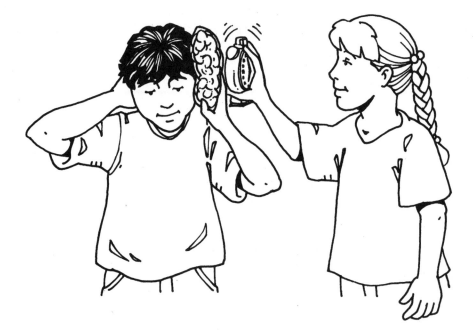

Step 1: Fill one bag with cotton. Seal the bag.

Step 2: Fill the other bag with air. Seal the bag.

Step 3: Hold the bag with cotton next to your ear. Ask a friend to hold the clock next to the bag. What do you hear?

Step 4: Hold the bag with air next to your ear. Ask a friend to hold the clock next to the bag. What do you hear?

When was the sound louder? Does sound travel better through cotton or air? What other things is it hard for sound to travel through?

YOUR EARS, P. 3
PUT ON YOUR THINKING CAP

Math Path

People who are deaf use sign language. They talk with their hands. Here are the hand signs for numbers.

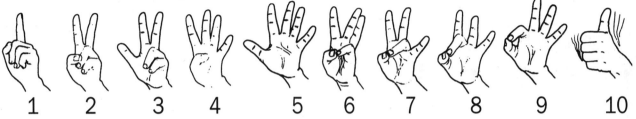

1   2   3   4   5   6   7   8   9   10

Directions: Write the answers to these problems. Then, sign the answers. Sign some new problems with a friend. Take turns.

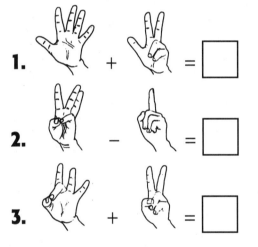

1.   +   = ☐

2.   −   = ☐

3.   +   = ☐

Vocabulary

Directions: How many words can you find hidden in HEARING-IMPAIRED? Write them on the lines below. The first one is done for you.

_____ ear _____   _____   _____

_____   _____   _____

_____   _____   _____

Your score: 3 words—O.K.   5 words—Good!   8 or more words—SUPER!

YOUR EARS, P. 4
FIGURE IT OUT!

People who are deaf use sign language. Here are the signs for finger spelling.

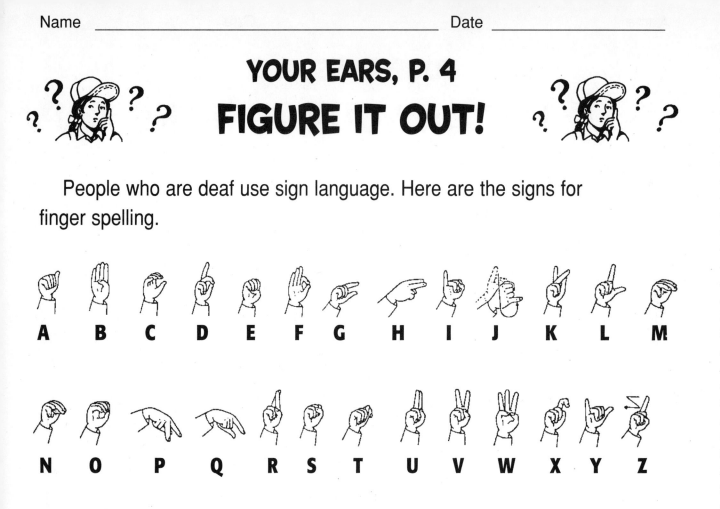

🔍 **Directions:** Use hand signs to spell your name. Say hello to a friend with hand signs. What else can you say with your hands?

BONUS: Do you use the Internet? Find out what's new in the world of science. Go to this address: **http://www.scienceweekly.com**

YOUR NOSE

You smell and **breathe** with your nose. To smell something, you need to **sniff** it. When you sniff, more air enters your nose. A smell is really tiny **particles** that float in the air. The smell moves with the air into your nose.

The air travels up to tiny **hairs** inside your nose. The tiny hairs pick up the smell. The hairs send a message to your brain. Your brain then **decides** what smell you have sniffed.

Your senses of smell and taste often work together. Your sense of smell helps you to know how food tastes. When you have a cold, you cannot taste food well. You have a **mucus lining** inside your nose. This lining gets thick when you have a cold. The thick mucus covers the tiny hairs. Then, the hairs cannot pick up smells.

YOUR NOSE, P. 2
LAB TIME

How much do you use your sense of smell? How do you know what is near you? What if you can't see it or hear it or feel it? Let's find out.

You will need: 3 mystery smells. (Keep these hidden.)

Step 1: Divide into small groups.

Step 2: Pick a leader. The leader will tell the others when to close their eyes. Close your eyes tightly. No peeking!

Step 3: The leader will pick one of the mystery smells.

Step 4: Then, the leader will hold the mystery smell under your nose.

Step 5: Try to guess the mystery smell. Don't say your answer out loud.

Step 6: After everyone has a turn, the leader will tell you to open your eyes.

How did you do? Did you guess all the smells? Are some smells easier to guess than others?

YOUR NOSE, P. 3
PUT ON YOUR THINKING CAP

Math Path

🔍 **Directions:** People like different smells. Students were asked about their favorite smell. Their answers are in the chart. Study the chart. Then, answer the questions.

Favorite Smell	Girls age 6	Girls age 9	Boys age 6	Boys age 9
strawberry	4	1	3	0
orange	1	6	1	4

1. How many students liked strawberry best?_____

2. How many liked orange best? _____

3. What smell did the girls like best?_____

4. What smell did the boys like best?_____

Science Words

🔍 **Directions:** Unscramble the "s" words that tell about your nose.

1. Your nose can _____ (**lesml**) a rose.

2. You _____ (**eznese**) when you have a cold.

3. You _____ (**finsf**) when you need to smell something.

4. Your nose gets _____ (**dtsufef**) up when you have a cold.

YOUR NOSE, P. 4
FIGURE IT OUT!

Animals have different kinds of noses. Some animals use their noses to find food. Other animals use their noses to keep them safe.

Directions: Look at these pictures of animals and their noses. Draw a line from the nose to the way it is used.

1.

hunting other animals

2.

digging up roots

3.

finding insects and worms

YOUR SENSE OF TOUCH

Your sense of touch tells about the things you touch. It also tells you about **temperature**, pain, and **pressure**.

Your skin is your largest **sense organ**. In your skin are **nerve** endings. The nerves gather information about touch. They send a message to the **spinal cord**. Then, the message moves to the brain. The brain sends **signals** to the body. The signals tell the body how to react.

Suppose you touch a hot pan. Nerves get the information of heat. They send the message to the spinal cord. The spinal cord sends the message to the brain. The brain tells your body to move away from the heat. If you could not feel the heat or the pain, your body would get hurt easily.

YOUR SENSE OF TOUCH, P. 2
LAB TIME

The skin on your fingers has many nerves. These nerves help you to feel things better. How well do you feel things with your fingers? Let's find out.

You will need: paper bag, 5 mystery things

Step 1: Put the mystery things in the bag. Don't show the things to anyone.

Step 2: Have a friend feel one thing in the bag. Ask the friend to tell about the thing. Is it hard, soft, round, or smooth?

Step 3: Ask your friend to guess what the thing is.

Step 4: Have other friends try to guess something in the bag.

Were your friends able to guess the things without looking? Who has the best sense of touch?

YOUR SENSE OF TOUCH, P. 3
PUT ON YOUR THINKING CAP

Touch Time

🔍 **Directions:** Look at the first picture in each row. How does it feel? Circle the other one in the row that feels the same.

YOUR SENSE OF TOUCH, P. 4
FIGURE IT OUT!

You have many nerves in your fingertips. So your fingers have a good sense of touch. The skin of your fingertips has another purpose. It can be used to tell who you are. Look at your fingertips. They have a special pattern of lines and spaces. These patterns are called fingerprints.

Here's an easy way to study your fingerprints. Press your thumb on an ink pad. Roll it slightly from side to side. Then, put one side of your inky thumb on some paper. Roll your thumb to the other side. Practice until you get a good print.

Then, get two pieces of paper. Label one piece "left hand." Label the other piece "right hand." Now, make fingerprints for all your fingers. Use a magnifying glass to study your fingerprints.

The lines in all fingerprints make three kinds of patterns. Look at the pictures of those patterns. What kind of patterns do you have? Compare your fingerprints with those of your classmates. Are your fingerprints exactly the same as anyone else's?

Arches	**Loops**	**Whorls**

MEMORY

When is your birthday? What letters are in your name? What is your telephone number? Your brain helps you to **remember** these things. Your memory is very **important**. Without it, you could not read or count. You could not even find your classroom. You would have to learn to do everything over and over.

You use your memory all the time. Your five senses help you to remember things. How does pizza taste and smell? What does thunder sound like? How does cool water feel? Your brain also helps you to remember **facts**. How much is 2 + 2? You remember. You remember how to do things, too. You remember how to tie your shoes or ride a bike.

Computers can do lots of things. They can spell words and do math. They can keep, or **store**, lots of facts. When you need the facts again, the computer **recalls** them. Your brain is like a computer. It can store facts and recall them quickly. This is your memory.

MEMORY, P. 2
LAB TIME

Your brain is amazing. Your memory is amazing, too. The more you use it, the better it works. How good is your memory? Let's find out.

You will need: paper, pencil, clock or stopwatch

List A	List B	List C
tah	hat	The
atc	cat	fat
taf	fat	cat
ats	sat	sat
		on
		the
		hat.

Step 1: Work with a partner. Your partner will take the memory test first. You will check the time.

Step 2: First, cover up all three lists. Then, let your partner look at List A for 1 minute. After 1 minute, cover up all the lists again.

Step 3: Now, your partner must write down everything he or she remembers from List A.

Step 4: Then, uncover List A again. Check what your partner has written. How much did he or she remember?

Step 5: Repeat Steps 2 through 4 with List B. Then, repeat the steps with List C.

Step 6: When your partner has done all three lists, change places. You will take the memory test. Your partner will check the time.

Which list was the hardest to remember? Which list was the easiest to remember? Why?

MEMORY, P. 3
PUT ON YOUR THINKING CAP

Science Words

🔍 **Directions:** There are six terms about memory in **dark print** on page 27. Look back at the page. Write down the six terms in a list. Study the list for 1 minute. Then, cover the list. Now, as quickly as possible, write as many of the six terms as you can remember.

_____   _____

_____   _____

_____   _____

How well did you do?

✏️ Writing About Science

🔍 **Directions:** What things can you remember? Complete each sentence.

1. My birthday is _____.

2. I had _____ for dinner last night.

3. I got _____ for my birthday last year.

MEMORY, P. 4
FIGURE IT OUT!

Sometimes our brain plays tricks on us. It doesn't want to recall what we want it to. Try this activity to test your brain.

First, color in the tip of each crayon. The Key tells you what color to use. Then, use that color of crayon to darkly color in all the letters of that word.

Now, out loud, name the color each word is filled in with. Do **not** read what the word says. Try this a few times. How did you do? What is your brain remembering?

Key	1–blue	2–green	3–yellow	4–red	5–black	6–brown

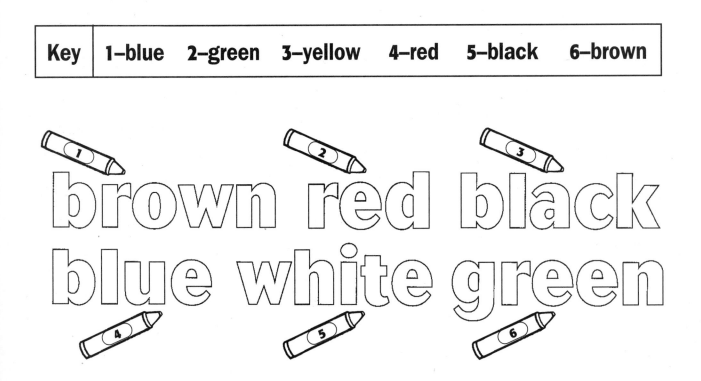

Did your brain trick you? Did it want to say the word instead of the color?

SLEEP AND DREAMS

Do you like to sleep? All living **creatures** must sleep or **rest** every day. People, fish, and even the smallest insects need **daily** sleep or rest. Sleep gives the body a chance to rest. Without sleep, the body would be too tired to work right.

What happens during sleep? While you are sleeping, you are **unconscious**. You do not know what is happening around you. Your body keeps working while you sleep. But most body **functions** slow down. Your breathing becomes slower. So does the beating of your heart. Your **body temperature** drops. That is why you need a cover or blanket when you sleep.

People also need to dream. Scientists think that dreams help your brain get ready to learn. Dreams may also make your memory better. Most people have three to six dreams each night. The first dream is the shortest. It might only be a few minutes long. The last dream is the longest. It might last 45 minutes.

SLEEP AND DREAMS, P. 2
LAB TIME

The pumping of your heart speeds up when you exercise. It slows down when you rest or sleep. Does your breathing speed up when you exercise? Does it slow down when you rest? Let's find out.

You will need: clock with second hand, pencil

Step 1: Sit in a chair and relax. Use the clock. Count the number of times you breathe in during 1 minute.

Step 2: Write the number in the chart.

Step 3: Now, run in place for 1 minute.

Step 4: Sit down again. Quickly count the number of times you breathe in during 1 minute.

Step 5: Write the number in the chart.

Step 6: Compare the number of breaths written in the chart.

Activity	Number of Breaths in 1 Minute
Resting	
Exercising	

What does your chart show? Do you breathe in more when you rest or when you exercise?

SLEEP AND DREAMS, P. 3
PUT ON YOUR THINKING CAP

Math Path

🔍 **Directions:** We all need different amounts of sleep. Use the bar graph to help you to answer the questions.

1. Who needs the most sleep each night?

_____

2. How many hours of sleep does an adult need each night?

_____

3. Does a 7-year-old or an adult need more sleep each night?

_____

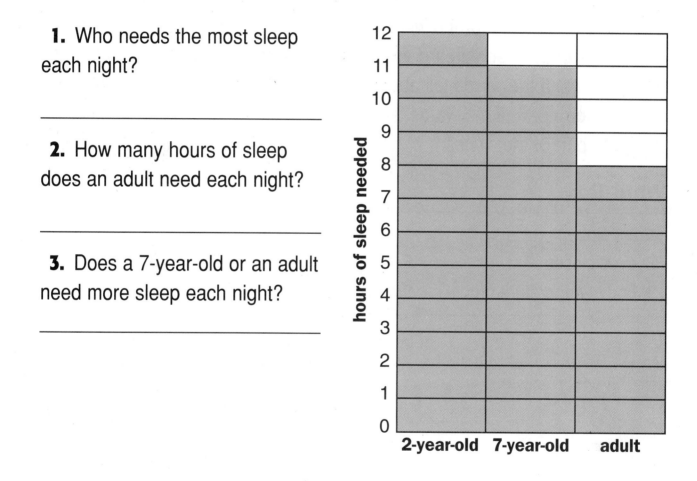

✏️ Writing About Science

Everybody needs sleep. Pretend that you have a friend who does not like to go to bed. Write a letter to this friend. Explain why sleep and dreams are important.

SLEEP AND DREAMS, P. 4
FIGURE IT OUT!

Is sleeping like being awake? Do your body and brain work the same both times? Look at the two circles below. You will use them to tell about when you are asleep and awake. Read the words in the Word Box. Do they tell about when you are awake, asleep, or both?

Write the numbers for the words in the correct part of the circles. If the words tell about when you are awake, write the number in the **Awake** part of the circles. If the words tell about when you are asleep, write the number in the **Asleep** part. If the words tell about both times, write the number in the **Both** part of the circles.

Word Box

1. eyes open	**4.** body organs work	**7.** dreams
2. eyes closed	**5.** body functions slow down	**8.** daydreams
3. body temperature drops	**6.** unconscious	

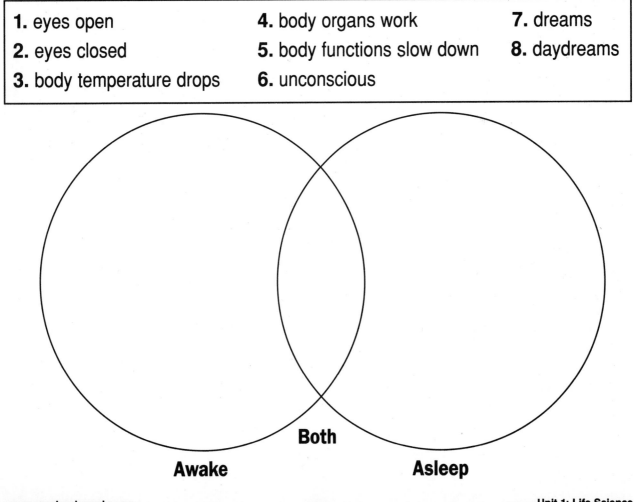

Both

Awake   Asleep

UNIT 2 ASSESSMENT

🔍 **Directions:** Darken the circle by the answer that correctly completes each statement.

1. Clouds are made of drops of _____.
   - Ⓐ water
   - Ⓑ ink
   - Ⓒ air

2. A _____ is a storm that brings heavy rains, high winds, and big waves.
   - Ⓐ blizzard
   - Ⓑ hurricane
   - Ⓒ tornado

3. Acid rain is caused by _____.
   - Ⓐ pollution
   - Ⓑ bicycles
   - Ⓒ snow

4. A storm with a funnel shape is a _____.
   - Ⓐ hurricane
   - Ⓑ blizzard
   - Ⓒ tornado

5. A _____ is a long period of not enough rain.
   - Ⓐ hurricane
   - Ⓑ drought
   - Ⓒ tornado

6. The top layer of the Earth is called the _____.
   - Ⓐ core
   - Ⓑ crust
   - Ⓒ dough

7. A sudden movement in the Earth's crust is _____.
   - Ⓐ a tornado
   - Ⓑ a volcano
   - Ⓒ an earthquake

8. The melted rock that flows from a volcano is called _____.
   - Ⓐ lightning
   - Ⓑ lava
   - Ⓒ glue

UNIT 2 SCIENCE FAIR IDEAS

The science fair is coming! You can learn more about the world you live in. What would you like to learn about? Use the scientific method. Follow these steps.

1. Problem: How much rain falls, and how can I tell?

2. Hypothesis: I think 1 inch of rain will fall when it rains.

3. Experimentation: Make a rain gauge to measure the rainfall. You will need a clear jar with straight sides, a ruler, a bucket, and tape. Tape the ruler on the inside of the jar, so it touches one side. Put the jar in the bucket outside in the rain. After it rains, look at the jar.

4. Observation: Some rain water is in the jar.

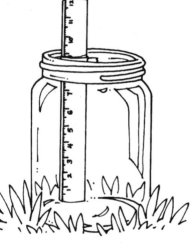

5. Conclusion: My homemade rain gauge measured the rain that fell in my yard. The rain measured $\frac{1}{2}$ inch on the ruler.

6. Comparison: I was not right to predict 1 inch of rain, but some rain fell. I learned how to collect and measure rainfall. I also learned it is hard to predict how much rain will fall in any one place.

7. Presentation: I can do the experiment on the playground at school. I can draw a picture of my rain gauge and tell how it works.

8. Resources: Tell the books you used to learn about rainfall and rain gauges. Tell who helped you to make the rain gauge.

Other Project Ideas ~~~~~~~~~~~~~~~~~~~~~~~~~~~~~~~~~

1. What causes fog to form?

2. How warm is it under the snow?

3. What causes an earthquake? Where do most earthquakes occur?

CLOUDS

Have you ever watched the clouds go by? Clouds can have many shapes. They can be thin or thick. They can look like funny animals.

How do clouds form? First, water on the Earth **evaporates**. It becomes **water vapor**. Water vapor is like warm, damp air. The water vapor rises. As it rises, it cools. Water **droplets** form. The droplets join together to make clouds. The water droplets grow bigger. Soon, they cannot be held up by the rising air. Then, they may fall as rain. The cloud may be cold and full of ice crystals. Then, snow may fall instead of rain.

There are three main kinds of clouds. **Cirrus clouds** are thin and high in the sky. They are usually seen in fair weather. **Cumulus clouds** are white and fluffy. They look like cotton balls. They are often seen in good weather. But they can cause rain showers or snow. **Stratus clouds** are low, dark clouds. They often make rain or snow.

CLOUDS, P. 2
LAB TIME

Clouds form when warm water vapor meets cool air. The water vapor changes into water droplets. The water droplets join to make a cloud. Do you think you can make a cloud in a bottle? Let's find out.

You will need: a wide-mouthed jar, plastic bowl, ice cubes, hot water

Step 1: Slowly fill the jar about half full with very hot water. Be careful. Get an adult to help you.

Step 2: Place the ice cubes in the plastic bowl. Put the bowl on the opening of the jar. Then, put the jar in the sunlight.

Step 3: Watch what happens inside the bottle. What do you see inside the bottle above the water?

The air above the hot water is warm and damp. It holds a lot of water vapor. What happens when the warm, damp air rises toward the ice cubes? What happens when warm, damp air is cooled? What forms when droplets of water float in the air?

Do you think the temperature is hot or cold where clouds form? Why?

CLOUDS, P. 3
PUT ON YOUR THINKING CAP

Science Words

🔍 **Directions:** Circle the correct word to finish each sentence.

1. Rain comes from _____.

    clothes   **clouds**   **clowns**

2. Clouds are made of tiny drops of _____.

    water   **fire**   **cotton**

3. Clouds look _____ when it rains.

    green   **white**   **dark**

Time to Think

You can predict the weather! Make a chart like the one below. Make the weather chart for five days of the week.

Draw pictures that show different kinds of weather. Weather can be sunny, cloudy, windy, rainy, or snowy.

Today, guess what the weather will be like tomorrow. Put a picture of that weather on the chart. Tomorrow, put a picture under your guess to show what the weather really is like.

Do this each day for one week. How many times were you right?

Our Weather				
Monday	Tuesday	Wednesday	Thursday	Friday
we think / we think	we think			

CLOUDS, P. 4
FIGURE IT OUT!

🔍 **Directions:** Show the way clouds are made. Cut out the pictures. Paste them in the boxes. Start with the top box.

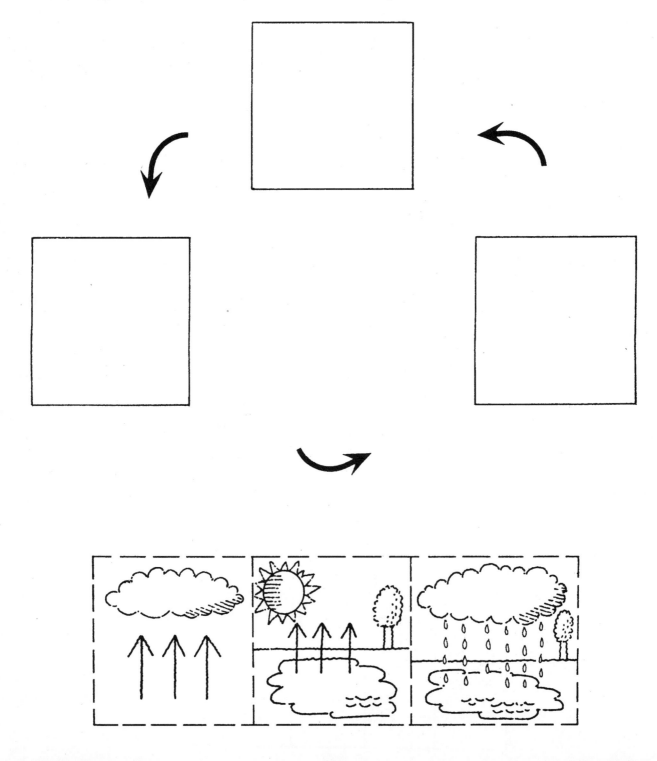

HURRICANES

CLUSTER OF THUNDERSTORMS   TROPICAL STORM   HURRICANE

Hurricanes are big **storms** with strong winds. They bring lots of rain. Hurricane winds blow in big circles like giant pinwheels. The winds blow at least 74 **miles per hour**. That's much faster than a school bus moves!

June to November is called **hurricane season**. Hurricanes begin over warm ocean water. Then, they move toward the **coast**. Some hurricanes never reach the land. But it is often hard to guess where they will go.

If hurricanes reach the land, they can cause much **damage**. The heavy rains flood the land. The strong winds rip at trees and buildings. Most hurricanes do not last long once they reach land. They lose **energy** and die.

HURRICANES, P. 2
LAB TIME

A hurricane has very strong winds. These winds can damage houses and buildings. What would happen if a hurricane struck a city? Let's find out.

You will need: milk cartons, scissors, glue, paper, markers, small dish, water, hair dryer or fan

---

Step 1: You are going to build a city using milk cartons. You will need an adult to help you with this experiment.

Step 2: Use the milk cartons and other supplies to make buildings. Line up the buildings to make streets.

Step 3: Then, blow gently on the buildings. This is like a light wind. What happens to the buildings?

Step 4: Next, blow harder on the buildings. This is like a strong wind. What happens to the buildings?

Step 5: Finally, the adult will turn on the hair dryer or fan. This is like hurricane winds. What happens to the buildings this time?

What happens with different wind speeds? Write a short report about this experiment.

HURRICANES, P. 3
PUT ON YOUR THINKING CAP

Math Path

🔍 **Directions:** Solve these problems about Hurricane Bob.

1. Hurricane Bob lasted for 3 days. The storm traveled 10 miles on Monday. It moved 15 miles on Tuesday. It went 20 miles on Wednesday. How many miles did Bob travel in all?

_____ miles

2. On Monday, Bob's wind speed was 80 miles per hour. By Tuesday, the wind speed was 100 miles per hour. How much faster was Bob's wind speed on Tuesday?

_____ miles per hour

✏️ Writing About Science

Pretend that a hurricane is coming your way. Remember that hurricanes have strong winds and heavy rains. Look at the picture. What can be done to stop hurricane damage? On another sheet of paper, make a list of things that should be done.

HURRICANES, P. 4
FIGURE IT OUT!

Scientists watch hurricanes and name them. They warn people when a hurricane is coming. Then, people have time to get ready or to leave.

Many hurricanes start in the Atlantic Ocean. Find the Atlantic Ocean on the map. Color it **blue**. An Atlantic hurricane could strike the coast anywhere from Texas to Maine. Find these areas on the map. Color them **green**.

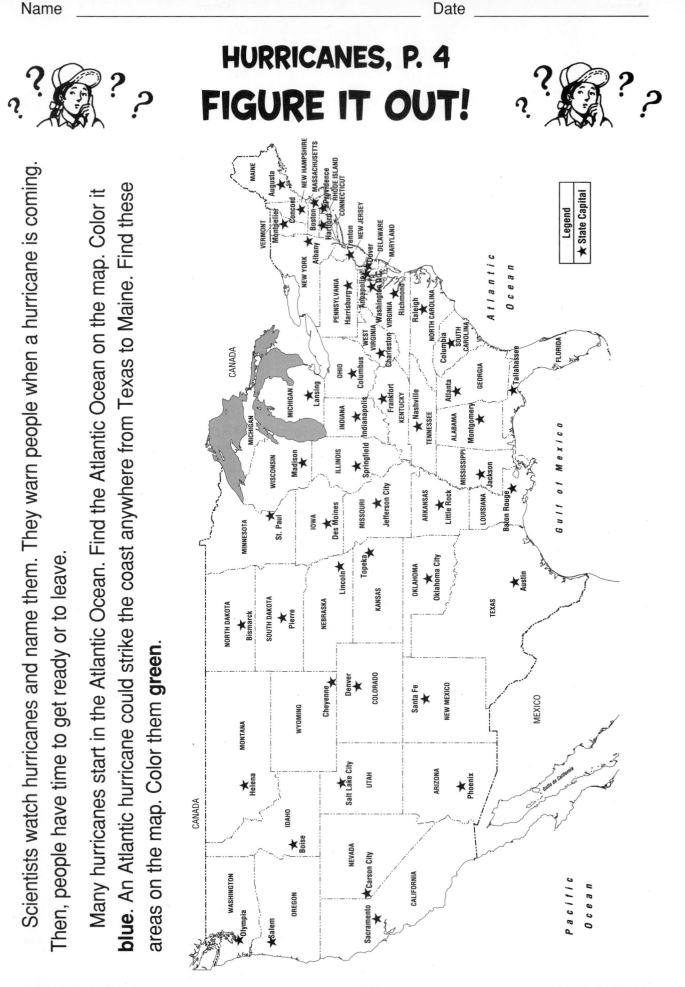

Legend
★ State Capital

TORNADOES

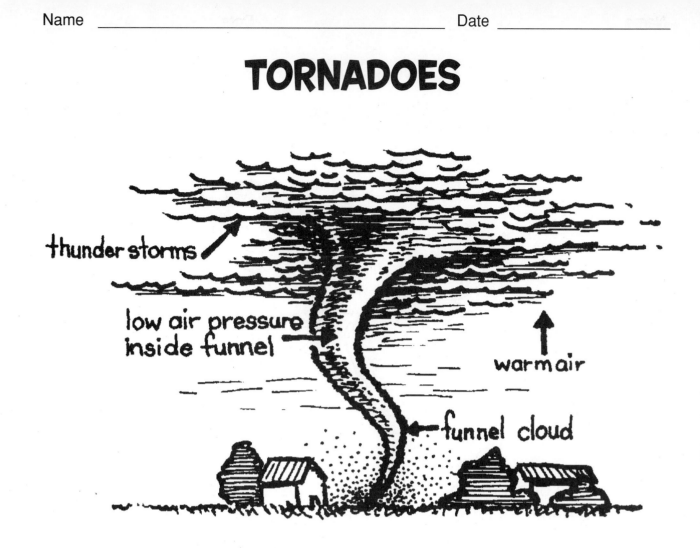

What happens in a **storm**? The clouds get dark. Then, **lightning** flashes, and thunder crashes. One of the dark clouds may turn into a **funnel** shape. It may become a tornado.

Tornadoes usually happen only in the **central** United States. They usually form in the spring or summer. Cool air moves down from the north. Warm air moves up from the south. The cool air bumps into the warm air. A funnel-shaped cloud starts. The winds begin to **swirl** around the funnel. A tornado has begun. The winds move very fast. They can blow up to 300 miles per hour. A tornado's winds are the fastest on Earth.

Most tornadoes are small. They don't travel very far. They cause little damage. Big tornadoes can smash buildings. They can rip up trees. They can carry cars and animals hundreds of feet in the air.

TORNADOES, P. 2
LAB TIME

The winds of a tornado form a funnel shape. This shape looks like an elephant's trunk. You can make a "tornado in a bottle." Here's how.

You will need: an empty 2-liter soft drink bottle, water, food coloring, liquid soap

Step 1: Fill the bottle about $\frac{3}{4}$ full with water.

Step 2: Add a few drops of food coloring and liquid soap.

Step 3: Put the cap on the bottle. Close the bottle tightly.

Step 4: Move the bottle in a circle. See the picture.

What happens in the bottle? How is the swirling water like a tornado?

BONUS: Do you have Internet service? Try visiting the Science Weekly web site. See what's new in the world of science. Go to this address: **www.scienceweekly.com**

TORNADOES, P. 3
PUT ON YOUR THINKING CAP

Science Words

🔍 **Directions:** Put the words in the box in alphabetical order.

funnel	thunder	lightning	storm

1. _____

2. _____

3. _____

4. _____

✏️ Writing About Science

Pretend that you are a reporter for the Tornado Times. On another sheet of paper, write a news story. Use one of these headlines:

Cows Blow Away

Pigs Seen Flying

Biggest Storm in the World

House, Girl, and Dog Picked Up by Tornado

Don't forget to draw a picture for your front-page story!

TORNADOES, P. 4
FIGURE IT OUT!

Scientists can predict the weather. They can tell when tornadoes are coming. They can tell when other kinds of weather will happen, too.

Directions: Look at the pictures in the map key. They stand for each kind of weather. Make your own weather map. Draw pictures of the different kinds of weather on the map. Then, get another piece of paper. Write a weather report about your map.

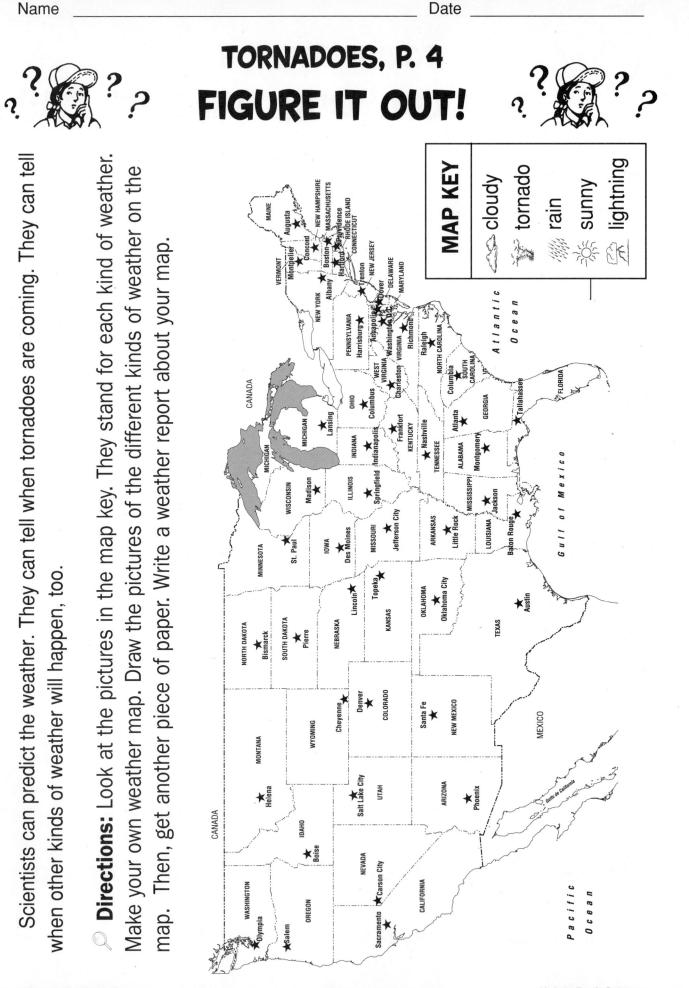

MAP KEY

cloudy	
tornado	
rain	
sunny	
lightning	

Name _____ Date _____

ACID RAIN

Does a rainy day make you sad because you cannot play outdoors? Rain is important to all living things. Rain refills rivers, streams, and lakes. Plants and animals need the rain's water to live and grow.

Not all rain is good for living things. Some rain contains **poisons**. This kind of rain is called **acid rain**. Acid rain hurts living things. Acid rain damages the **environment**.

What makes acid rain? Air **pollution** can change rain into acid rain. **Fumes** from factories, cars, and power plants **pollute** the air. Pollution smells bad and causes acid rain.

Acid rain harms forests. Leaves may fall off trees. The bark may be damaged, too. The trees may stop growing. Acid rain can also harm lakes, rivers, and streams. Then, the animals in the water are hurt, too.

ACID RAIN, P. 2
LAB TIME

Plants need clean, fresh water to grow. An acid changes the water. It makes the water sour. Will a bean seed sprout in a weak acid? Let's find out.

You will need: 4 lima bean seeds, 2 clear plastic cups, paper towels, water, vinegar, plastic wrap

Step 1: Label one cup **WATER** and one cup **VINEGAR**. (Vinegar is a weak acid.) Put a piece of paper towel on the inside of each cup.

Step 2: In each cup, place two bean seeds between the cup and the paper towel. Look at the picture to see how to do this.

Step 3: Put some water in the cup labeled WATER. Do not cover the seeds with water.

Step 4: Repeat Step 3 with vinegar. Pour some vinegar in the cup labeled VINEGAR.

Step 5: Cover both cups with plastic wrap. Place the cups in the sunlight. Watch the seeds for one week.

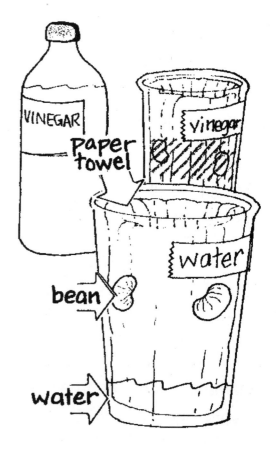

What happens to the seeds when they get wet? Do the seeds in the water begin to grow? Do the seeds in the acid begin to grow? Why is it important to stop acid rain?

ACID RAIN, P. 3
PUT ON YOUR THINKING CAP

✏️ Writing About Science

🔍 **Directions:** Write three sentences about acid rain. Use some of the words in the clouds.

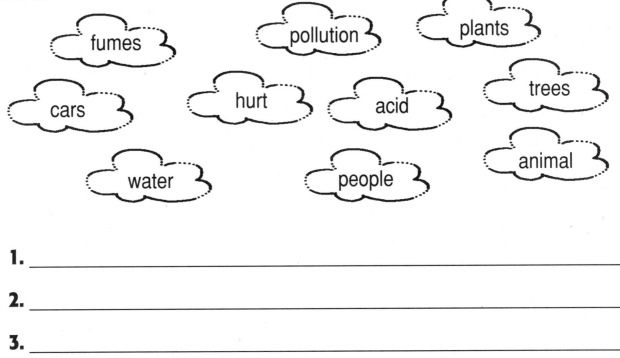

1. _____

2. _____

3. _____

Time to Think

How can acid rain be stopped? We must work to stop air pollution. We must use less oil, gasoline, and coal. We must use other kinds of transportation that pollute less.

You can help to stop acid rain and air pollution! Starting a car pool or riding the bus is one way. Walking or riding a bike is another way.

Design a colorful poster. Tell people to use car pools and buses. Tell them to walk or ride bikes. Include a catchy slogan.

ACID RAIN, P. 4
FIGURE IT OUT!

Pollution is something that spoils a habitat. Smoke in the air is pollution. Oil in the water is pollution. A tire in a stream is pollution. Litter is pollution, too.

People cause pollution problems. People can solve pollution problems, too. They help by cleaning up trash. They help by picking up litter. They help by making their world cleaner.

Directions: Look at the picture. Circle the kinds of pollution people can clean up in the park.

DROUGHT

Water is important to all kinds of life. Sometimes a place does not get enough rain for a long time. Then, the place has a drought. Plants and crops do not get the water they need. They can dry up and die. Even animals and people can die in a bad drought.

During a drought, people cannot water their lawns. They cannot wash their cars. Many swimming pools are closed. Every drop of water must be **conserved**.

The summer of 1988 was very hot and dry. That summer, much of the United States was in a drought. There was not enough rain for corn and wheat to grow tall. The **thirsty** plants dried up.

Farmers even wished **weeds** would grow. The **roots** of weeds help keep the **topsoil** from blowing away. Topsoil has food in it to help plants grow. Without topsoil, a farm can quickly become like a **desert**.

DROUGHT, P. 2
LAB TIME

Water is our most important resource. People need water to stay alive. Do plants need water to stay alive? Let's find out.

You will need: celery with leaves, 2 large clear cups, water

Step 1: Label the cups **Cup 1** and **Cup 2**.

Step 2: Have an adult cut two stalks of celery. Place one stalk in Cup 1 and one stalk in Cup 2. Do not add water to the jars. Leave them overnight.

Step 3: Look at the celery stalks the next day. What do they look like? Draw a picture of the stalks, and write about how they look.

Step 4: Leave the stalks in the jar. Now, add water to Cup 1. Do not add water to Cup 2. Leave the two cups overnight.

Step 5: Look at the celery stalks the next day. Do the two stalks look the same? Draw a picture of the two stalks, and write about how they look.

Step 6: Add water to Cup 2 after seven days.

What do the two stalks look like the next day? Do the stalks look the same? Can water always bring a plant back to life?

DROUGHT, P. 3
PUT ON YOUR THINKING CAP

Math Path

🔍 **Directions:** Study the chart about grain prices. Then, answer the questions.

Grain	Price per Bag
corn	$3.00
wheat	$4.00
soybeans	$10.00
oats	$3.50

1. Which grain costs the most per bag? _____

2. How much will 3 bags of corn cost? _____

3. How much will 10 bags of wheat cost? _____

4. How much will 2 bags of oats cost? _____

5. How much will 4 bags of corn and 3 bags of wheat cost? _____

✏️ Writing About Science

Pretend that a drought has struck your area. Rain has not fallen for over three months. Your family needs to conserve water. Get another piece of paper. Make a list of ten things that you can do at your home to save water. Then, tell how you would feel if you did not have enough water to use.

DROUGHT, P. 4
FIGURE IT OUT!

🔍 **Directions:** Use the picture clues to complete the puzzle.

EARTHQUAKES

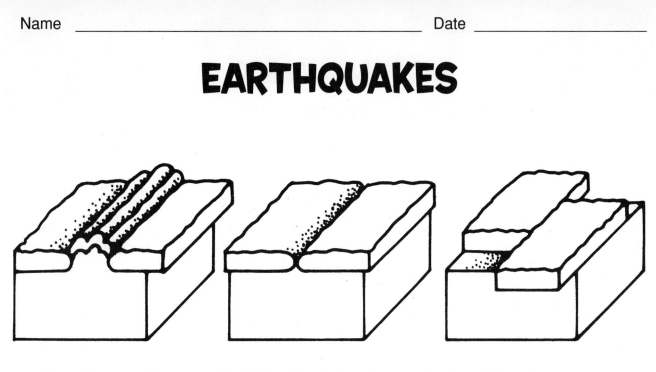

Rumble, rumble, rumble! The Earth begins to shake. What is happening?

The outer part of the Earth is called the **crust**. The **ground** we stand on feels solid. But it is really made up of huge pieces of the crust. The huge pieces are called **plates**. These plates are always moving very slowly **underground**. The plates may bump into each other. When they do, the ground moves. The ground may crack, shake, or roll. This is an earthquake!

There are almost a **million** earthquakes each year. Most of them are very small. We don't even feel the shaking from these small earthquakes. If the crust moves quickly and suddenly, a big earthquake can happen.

Big earthquakes send **shock waves** over hundreds of miles. The shock waves cause the Earth's crust to shake and roll. These movements can cause much damage. Buildings and bridges may fall down.

EARTHQUAKES, P. 2
LAB TIME

Scientists work on new ways to make buildings safer. They want to stop damage to buildings during earthquakes. They add cross-beams to the buildings. They also use steel braces. These things make buildings stronger. Can you make a building strong enough for an earthquake? Let's find out.

> **You will need:** blocks, plastic straws, tape, scissors, construction paper

Step 1: Lay a piece of construction paper on the table. On the paper, stack four to eight blocks to make a building.

Step 2: Carefully shake the paper from side to side. Watch for any damage to your building. What happened to your building?

Step 3: Make the building again. This time, tape two straws to the corners of your building. Make X-beams with the straws. Do this at both ends.

Step 4: Carefully shake the paper from side to side again. What happened to your building this time? Was there as much damage?

Make other kinds of buildings. Put them through the earthquake test. What kind of damage do they have? How else can you make your buildings stronger?

EARTHQUAKES, P. 3
PUT ON YOUR THINKING CAP

Science Words

🔍 **Directions:** Look at the words in the box. Each word fits into one of the building shapes. Write the correct word in each shape.

crust	plates	shock

1.

2.

3.

✏️Writing About Science

Pretend that your home was damaged by an earthquake. Think about all your things. What would you want to save? Pretend that you have 15 minutes to go back into your damaged home. You have one shopping cart to fill. Write a story about what you would choose to save.

EARTHQUAKES, P. 4
FIGURE IT OUT!

The Earth is like a giant ball. It is made of three layers. The center of the Earth is called the core. It is very hot. The middle layer is called the mantle. It is wrapped around the core. The core heats the mantle. The mantle is so hot that some rocks in this layer melt. The outer layer is called the crust. It is solid and thinner than the other layers. The crust is made of rock and soil. We live on the crust of the Earth.

Pretend that a hard-boiled egg is the Earth. The thin eggshell is the crust. Gently tap the egg on a hard surface. The broken pieces of eggshell are the Earth's plates. All the land and oceans sit on top of these plates. Now, try to slide some pieces of shell over each other. Did the "plates" move smoothly, or was some force needed to move them?

Next, put a finger on top of the egg and your thumb on the bottom. Squeeze gently. Did any of the plates move up over other plates? The plates that rose up show how mountains are formed.

Finally, use a plastic knife to cut the egg in half. The egg yolk is the glowing core of the Earth, and the egg white is the mantle. The broken eggshell shows the plates of the Earth's crust.

🔍 **Directions:** Look at the picture. Label the three layers of the Earth.

1. _____

2. _____

3. _____

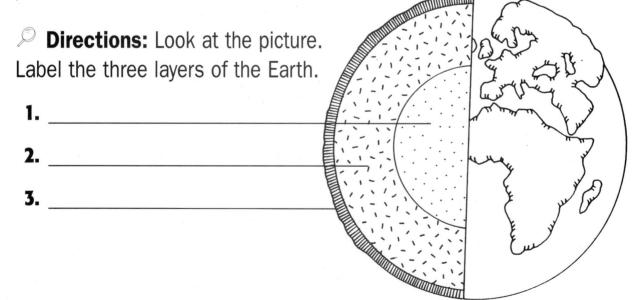

Name _____   Date _____

VOLCANOES

Black smoke rises into the air. Dust and **ash** darken the sky. Red-hot **lava** flows up from inside the Earth. A volcano has **erupted**!

The inside of the Earth is very hot. It is so hot that the rock in the Earth's **core** is melted. This melted rock is called **magma**. The outer part of the Earth is called the crust. The Earth's crust is made of cooled rock.

A volcano forms in steps. First, magma rises from the core. The magma makes a pool deep in the crust. Then, cracks form in the crust above the magma pool. The magma begins to move into the cracks. It slowly moves toward the surface. Sometimes the magma just oozes out onto the ground. Then, it is called lava.

Sometimes the volcano explodes. Rock, dust, and ash are thrown into the air. The magma flows out onto to the ground. This is called **lava flow**.

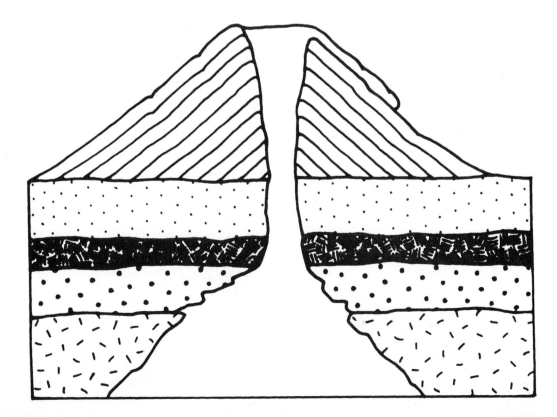

VOLCANOES, P. 2
LAB TIME

The part of the volcano above the Earth's surface is the cone. The top of the cone has an opening. Often a crater, shaped like a bowl, forms around the opening. How does a volcano erupt? Let's find out.

You will need: modeling clay, pencil, paper plate, baking soda, vinegar, red food coloring

---

Step 1: Shape the modeling clay into a cone about six inches tall. Do your work on the paper plate.

Step 2: Use the pencil to make a tunnel through the middle of the cone. Be careful. The tunnel should go from the top to the bottom.

Step 3: You might want to add a crater at the top of the cone. Make a small bowl-shaped hole with your thumb.

Step 4: Now, put about a teaspoon of baking soda into the tunnel and the crater of your volcano. Add a few drops of the red food coloring to the baking soda.

Step 5: Make sure you have the volcano on the paper plate. You might also put old newspaper around the paper plate.

Step 6: Finally, add three or four drops of vinegar to the baking soda. Stand back and watch your volcano erupt!

VOLCANOES, P. 3
PUT ON YOUR THINKING CAP

Word Search

🔍 **Directions:** Find the words in the box. Circle the letters that make each word.

core	magma	crust	Earth	melted	hot	volcano	lava

```
        O V L
        R C O R E
      A M E L T E D
      V L A V C R U S T
    A M A G M A Y W P C H
    C O V P J N K S A X O
    U E R A T H O V E A R T H
```

✏️ Writing About Science

Pretend that you go on a trip to the center of the Earth. What would you see on the way? How would you feel? What would the Earth's core look like? On another piece of paper, write a story that tells about your journey. Make a drawing for your story, too.

VOLCANOES, P. 4
FIGURE IT OUT!

Directions: Connect the dots. Begin at **Start**. Write the letter near each dot in the correct blank below. When you are finished, color the picture.

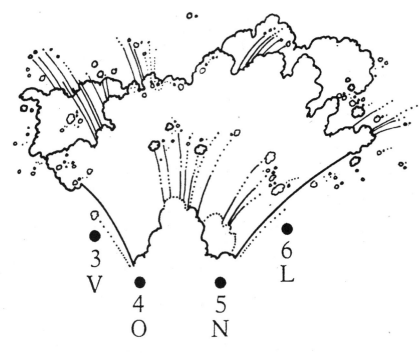

Start • 1
C

8
A

What do you see in the picture?

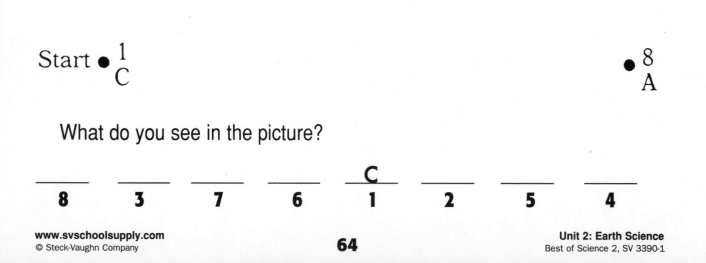

____ ____ ____ ____ C ____ ____ ____
8   3   7   6   1   2   5   4

UNIT 3 ASSESSMENT

🔍 **Directions:** Darken the circle by the answer that correctly completes each statement.

1. Cooks follow a _____ to prepare a food.
- Ⓐ poem
- Ⓑ bus
- Ⓒ recipe

2. The things used to make a cake are called _____.
- Ⓐ ingredients
- Ⓑ scientists
- Ⓒ rocks

3. A tiny plant used to make bread rise is _____.
- Ⓐ air
- Ⓑ yeast
- Ⓒ corn

4. Another name for corn is _____.
- Ⓐ maize
- Ⓑ rice
- Ⓒ wheat

5. The hard outer shell of popcorn is called the _____.
- Ⓐ crust
- Ⓑ hull
- Ⓒ skin

6. Most sugar is made from sugar cane or sugar _____.
- Ⓐ trees
- Ⓑ beets
- Ⓒ carrots

7. Chocolate is made from the beans of the _____.
- Ⓐ cacao tree
- Ⓑ candy bush
- Ⓒ peanut plant

8. A drinking straw is a small hollow _____.
- Ⓐ box
- Ⓑ hole
- Ⓒ tube

UNIT 3 SCIENCE FAIR IDEAS

The science fair is coming! You can learn more about the world you live in. What would you like to learn about? Use the scientific method. Follow these steps.

1. Problem: Does frozen water weigh the same as liquid water?

2. Hypothesis: Frozen water and liquid water weigh the same.

3. Experimentation: Do an experiment. Materials: one cup of water, self-sealing plastic bag, kitchen scale. Put the water into the bag. Weigh the bag of liquid water. Freeze the water. Weigh the bag of frozen water.

4. Observation: The frozen water and the liquid water have the same weight.

5. Conclusion: The amount of water stayed the same. Changing water from a liquid to a solid did not change its weight.

6. Comparison: The hypothesis and the conclusion agree.

7. Presentation: Put the bag of water and the scale on a table. Make a chart to show the weight of the water and the ice. Write a story to tell what you did.

8. Resources: Tell the books you used to find information. Tell who helped you get materials and set up the experiment.

Other Project Ideas ~~~~~~~~~~~~~~~~~~~~~~~~~~~~~

1. What are the little bubbles in a can of soda?

2. Can salt make foods sweeter?

3. What is the difference between a mixture and a solution?

KITCHEN SCIENCE

Did you know that you have a science **laboratory** right in your home? It's your kitchen! When you make things in your kitchen, you are using science. **Cooks** are a lot like scientists. Both of them mix things together to make something new.

Everything in the world is made of **chemicals**. When chemicals are mixed together, interesting things can happen. In laboratories, scientists mix chemicals. In kitchens, cooks mix chemicals, too. But cooks call them **ingredients**. A scientist does an experiment. A cook uses a **recipe**. Both need to follow directions and measure carefully.

Sometimes you can **combine** lots of ingredients to make a new thing. When you bake, you can mix flour, sugar, milk, and eggs with other good things. All of these things combine. They change to something new, such as a cake or cookies.

KITCHEN SCIENCE, P. 2
LAB TIME

Everything in the world is made of chemicals. In the kitchen, chemicals can change in many ways. They can be heated or cooled. They can be boiled or frozen. Powders dissolve in water. Vegetables are mixed to make a salad. Many of these changes are easy to see. Do you think the chemicals in foods can change a penny? Let's find out.

> **You will need:** 3 clear plastic cups, water, dill pickle juice, vinegar, salt, dull pennies

Step 1: Add 3 tablespoons of dill pickle juice to the first cup.

Step 2: Add 3 tablespoons of vinegar and 12 shakes of salt to the second cup.

Step 3: Add 3 tablespoons of water to the last cup.

Step 4: Put dull pennies in each cup.

Step 5: Watch what happens to the pennies.

dull pennies

vinegar and salt   dill pickle juice   water

What happened to the pennies? Did all the pennies turn shiny? Why do you think some pennies turned shiny and others did not?

BONUS: Do you have Internet service? Try visiting the <u>Science</u> <u>Weekly</u> web site. See what's new in the world of science. Go to this address: **www.scienceweekly.com**

KITCHEN SCIENCE, P. 3
PUT ON YOUR THINKING CAP

Math Path

🔍 **Directions:** Cooks need to measure carefully. Use the graph to answer the questions.

= 1 cup

pint

quart

$\frac{1}{2}$ gallon

1. How many cups are in a pint? _____

2. How many cups are in a quart? _____

3. How many cups are in $\frac{1}{2}$ gallon? _____

4. How many pints are in a quart? _____

5. How many quarts are in $\frac{1}{2}$ gallon? _____

✏️ Writing About Science

Pretend that you are in a cooking contest. You have to make the "Worst Sandwich in the World." On another piece of paper, write a story about your sandwich. List all the ingredients you would put in your sandwich. Don't forget to give your sandwich a name! Draw a picture of your sandwich.

KITCHEN SCIENCE, P. 4
FIGURE IT OUT!

Have you ever made a mixture? You may have mixed a vegetable salad or fruit salad. You may have mixed up some clothes in a drawer. A mixture is made when you combine several things.

The things that go into a mixture can be separated. You can take the different vegetables or fruits out of a salad. They will be the same as they were before. You can sort the clothes in a drawer. They will not have changed.

Directions: Separate the things in these mixtures. Draw them in different groups.

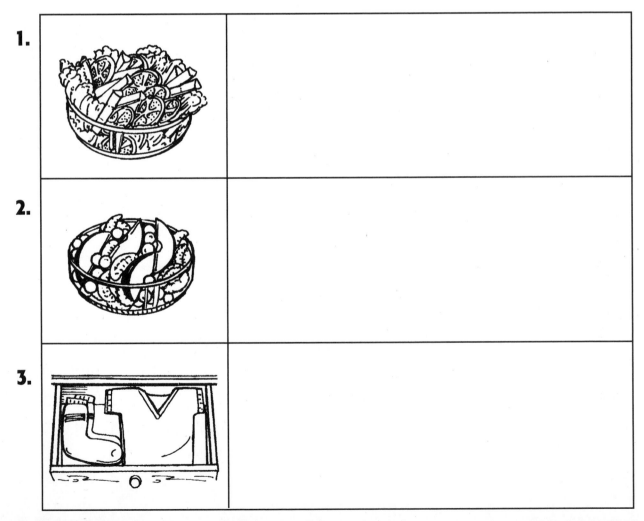

1.

2.

3.

THE SCIENCE OF COOKING

Do you like to cook? Have you ever baked cookies or a cake? Every time you cook something, you see science in action. Have you ever smelled bread baking? That **delicious** smell is caused by the **yeast** in the bread dough.

Yeast is a tiny plant. If you add sugar and warm water, the yeast plants grow. They give off tiny **gas bubbles**. These gas bubbles cause the bread dough to **expand**, or get bigger. The bread rises in the pan. Baking the bread stops the yeast plant from growing any more.

A cake batter rises, too. Why doesn't it smell like bread when it bakes? A cake does not contain yeast. Instead, its recipe calls for **baking powder**. Baking powder is a mixture of several chemicals. When baking powder touches water, it reacts. **Carbon dioxide** bubbles form. These gas bubbles make the cake rise.

THE SCIENCE OF COOKING, P. 2
LAB TIME

Do you like bread and cakes? Just imagine a fluffy slice of cake topped with ice cream. Have you ever tasted a cake that went flat? It is not fluffy at all. What makes bread and cake rise? Let's find out.

You will need: 1 package of active dry yeast, sugar, warm water, 2 teaspoons, 2 small bowls, baking powder

---

Step 1: Observe, feel, and smell the ingredients. Do you think they will be the same when you finish?

Step 2: Mix 1 package of yeast, 1 teaspoon of sugar, and $\frac{1}{4}$ cup of warm water in the first bowl. (Make sure the water is not too hot. If it is too hot, you will kill the yeast.) Set the bowl aside.

Step 3: Put 1 teaspoon of baking powder in the second bowl. Add warm water.

What happens in each bowl? Does everything happen right away? Why or why not? Are the ingredients the same at the end as at the beginning?

THE SCIENCE OF COOKING, P. 3
PUT ON YOUR THINKING CAP

Time to Think

🔍 **Directions:** Cross out the recipes that do not belong. Then, tell why.

Flour	Sand
Water	Yeast

Flour	Yeast
Water	Sugar

Water	Yeast
Sawdust	Sugar

_____

_____

_____

✏️ Writing About Science

🔍 **Directions:** Complete each sentence.

1. If I heat popcorn kernels in a pan, _____

_____.

2. If I heat cheese in a pan on the stove, _____

_____.

3. If I boil noodles in water, _____

_____.

THE SCIENCE OF COOKING, P. 4
FIGURE IT OUT!

When water freezes, it expands, or gets bigger. But most gases, solids, and liquids contract, or get smaller, when they are cooled. If you heat a balloon, it will expand. A sidewalk will contract if it is cooled.

1. This series of pictures shows a balloon that is being heated. Number the pictures from warmest to coolest (1, 2, 3).

2. In these pictures, a jar lid is being cooled. The other jar lid is being heated. Circle the picture that shows the lid that would be easier to take off.

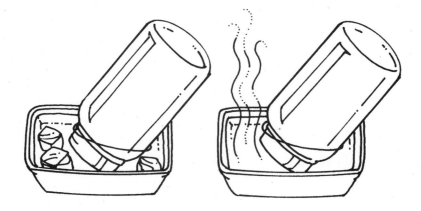

A-MAIZING CORN

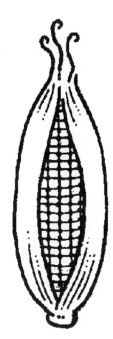

Do you like corn on the cob or corn bread? These foods have been eaten for a long time. Native Americans grew corn long before Columbus arrived. Corn, or **maize**, was their most important food.

How was corn used? Native Americans ate some **ears** fresh off the **stalk**. They dried other ears and stacked them for later use. Women used stones to grind the **kernels** into **cornmeal**. They used the cornmeal to make bread or **porridge**. They even made drinks from corn. One type of corn, popcorn, was a favorite snack!

Corn was used for other things, too. Dried kernels made good beads. They were also used as markers in games. The people made things from all parts of the corn stalk.
Nothing was wasted.

Will a dance help corn grow? Many Native American tribes thought so. The people danced and made music to help the corn to grow.

A-MAIZING CORN, P. 2
LAB TIME

Have you ever helped in a garden or on a farm? The soil must be prepared carefully. Otherwise, the crops will not grow well. Native Americans used digging sticks to plant corn. Do you know why? Let's find out.

You will need: craft sticks, 2 plastic cups, compacted soil, corn seeds

Step 1: First, the soil must be compacted. That means it is very hard and tightly packed.

Step 2: Break up half the soil with a craft stick. The soil should be soft and loose. Place it in a cup. Label this **Cup 1**.

Step 3: Place the other soil in the other cup. Do not break up this soil. It should remain hard and tightly packed. Label this **Cup 2**.

Step 4: Plant two or three corn seeds in each cup. The seeds should be about 1 inch below the surface of the soil. The seeds will be harder to plant in Cup 2.

Step 5: Keep the soil moist. Keep the cups away from direct sunlight.

Step 6: Observe the two cups every day.

In which cup do the plants grow faster? Why? Why is it a good idea to make the soil soft and loose? How does soft, loose soil help a plant to grow?

A-MAIZING CORN, P. 3
PUT ON YOUR THINKING CAP

Math Path

🔍 **Directions:** Native Americans put their corn in stacks. How many ears are in each stack?

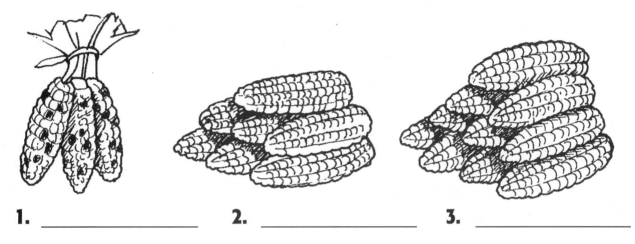

1. _____   2. _____   3. _____

Pattern Problem

🔍 **Directions:** Kernels of corn were used to make necklaces. Circle the group of beads that you can use to finish the necklace.

A-MAIZING CORN, P. 4
FIGURE IT OUT!

Native Americans told stories about corn. They drew a codex, or folding book, to show the story. Work with a partner. On another piece of paper, write a story. Your story can be about corn. It can also be about some other vegetable or plant. Then, draw a codex to illustrate the story.

POPCORN CHEMISTRY

Do you like to eat popcorn while watching TV or a movie? Popcorn is America's favorite snack food. It's a healthy snack, too. You can eat a lot and not get fat.

Have you ever wondered what makes popcorn pop? An uncooked kernel has two parts. The hard outer **shell** is called the **hull**. The soft **filling** is made mostly of **starch** and water. The hull keeps the water in. The amount of water in popcorn has to be just right. Otherwise, the popcorn will not pop. Cracked kernels do not pop. Too much water has dried up in them. Plain corn does not pop, either. The starch in plain corn is too wet. The hull is too soft, too.

When you cook popcorn, the water in the starch **boils**. Then, it turns to **steam**. The steam pushes on the hull. It pushes so hard that the hull pops like a balloon. The starch rushes out and expands. Let's eat!

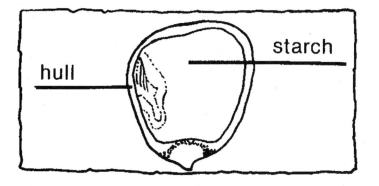

POPCORN CHEMISTRY, P. 2
LAB TIME

You know that popcorn gets bigger when it pops. How much bigger is popped popcorn than unpopped popcorn? Let's find out.

> **You will need:** some unpopped popcorn kernels, some popped popcorn, a piece of paper, a pencil, a centimeter ruler

Step 1: Get a pencil and paper. Trace around one unpopped kernel.

Step 2: Get a piece of popped popcorn.

Step 3: Trace around the popped popcorn.

Step 4: Use the ruler to measure the unpopped and popped popcorn.

_____ cm unpopped popcorn

_____ cm popped popcorn

Which is bigger? How much bigger? Did you know that two tablespoons of unpopped kernels make one liter of popped popcorn? That much popcorn only costs about ten cents to make. Best of all, popcorn is good for you.

POPCORN CHEMISTRY, P. 3
PUT ON YOUR THINKING CAP

Time to Think

🔍 **Directions:** Rosita, Juan, and Eva each have a different type of popcorn. Find out who has which type. Use the clues and the information in the first chart to help you. Write <u>yes</u> or <u>no</u> in each box in the second chart.

	White	**Yellow**	**Hybrid**
Size	small	medium	large
Taste	sweet	not sweet	sweet

Clue 1: Rosita's popcorn is not large, but it is sweet.

Clue 2: Juan's popcorn is not large.

What kind of popcorn does each person have?

	White	**Yellow**	**Hybrid**
Rosita			
Juan			
Eva			

✏️Writing About Science

Some Native Americans had stories about what made popcorn pop. They believed a little person lived in the popcorn. They thought that heating the popcorn made him mad. Then, he got so mad he blew up! Write your own story about what makes popcorn pop. Include a drawing for your story.

POPCORN CHEMISTRY, P. 4
FIGURE IT OUT!

Directions: Do you know how to pop popcorn? Look at the steps in the box. Then, put them in the right order in the flowchart. Use the number of each step to show the order. The first one is done for you.

1. Shake the pot.

2. Put the pot on the stove.

3. Add butter and salt.

4. Turn on the heat.

5. Eat.

6. Add $\frac{1}{4}$ cup of oil.

7. Pour the popcorn into a bowl.

8. Pour 1 cup of popcorn in the pot.

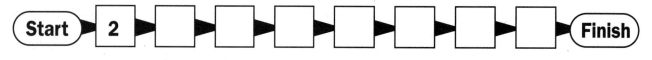

Start 2 ☐ ☐ ☐ ☐ ☐ ☐ ☐ Finish

An important step was left out. Do you know what it is?

BONUS: Draw a picture of yourself with a popcorn head. Write a short, silly poem to go with your picture.

SUGAR

Many of us have a "sweet tooth." We like sweet things. One of our favorite sweet things is sugar. It is in many foods that we eat each day. Did you know that most Americans eat about 36 **kilograms** of sugar each year? How much do you eat?

Where does sugar come from? Most of the sugar we eat comes from two plants. These two plants are **sugar cane** and **sugar beets**. Sugar cane grows best in very warm places. The sugar beet is a root vegetable. The part we eat is the root that grows under the ground. Sugar beets grow in a cooler **climate**.

Is sugar good for us? Sugar gives us quick energy. Our bodies **absorb** the energy from sugar easily. The energy is used up quickly. Sugar is not really a harmful crop. But too much of it in your diet can be harmful. It can cause tooth **decay** and other health problems.

SUGAR, P. 2
LAB TIME

Sugar can be used to make foods sweet. Do you think sugar can be used to keep things fresh? Let's find out.

> **You will need:** 3 fresh flowers, 3 cups, sugar, lemon-lime soda

Step 1: Fill two cups with water. Fill one cup with soda.

Step 2: Mix 1 teaspoon of sugar in one of the cups of water.

Step 3: Place one flower in each cup.

Step 4: Look at the flowers for seven days.

Which flowers lived the longest? Did the flower in water live as long as the flower in sugar water? Did the flower in water live as long as the flower in soda? Can you explain what happened?

BONUS: Do you have Internet service? Try visiting the Science Weekly web site. See what's new in the world of science. Go to this address: **www.scienceweekly.com**

SUGAR, P. 3
PUT ON YOUR THINKING CAP

Science Words

Directions: Draw a line to connect each word with its correct definition.

1. absorb   **a.** turning bad

2. kilogram   **b.** weather in a place

3. climate   **c.** to take in

4. decay   **d.** metric unit of weight

Writing About Science

Honey is sweet like sugar. The bear and the beekeeper are trying to get some honey. Write a story about their adventures. Which one do you think will succeed? Why?

_____

_____

_____

_____

_____

_____

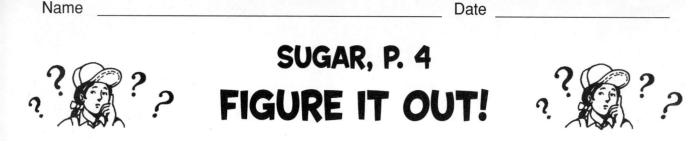

SUGAR, P. 4
FIGURE IT OUT!

A **solution** is a kind of mixture. It is made when a solid **dissolves** in a liquid. This means that the solid mixes with the liquid. Then, you cannot see the solid anymore. If the liquid is warm, the solid dissolves faster.

Let's make a solution. You will need two clear plastic cups, sugar, two teaspoons, warm water, ice-cold water, and a stopwatch. Put warm water in one cup. Put cold water in the other cup. Put 1 teaspoon of sugar in each cup. Put the sugar in the water at the same time. Stir each cup. Then, watch the sugar dissolve.

In which cup does the sugar dissolve first? Look at the stopwatch to see how long it took. Write down the time in seconds. When the sugar in the second cup dissolves, stop the stopwatch. Write down the time in seconds.

Make a graph using the two times you wrote down. Draw bars to show each time in seconds.

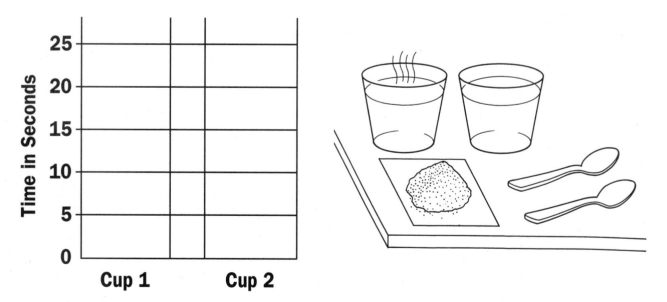

CHOCOLATE

What is white or purple, grows on trees, and tastes **bitter**? The answer is chocolate, before it becomes your favorite candy bar. Chocolate is made from the beans of the **cacao tree**. The cacao tree grows only in very warm places of the world. The beans grow inside football-shaped **pods**. Each pod holds about 50 beans. First, the beans are picked. Then, they are left to dry in the sun. Drying helps them to last longer. When the beans are dry, they are called **cocoa beans**. The cocoa beans are then sent to chocolate factories all around the world.

At the factories, the beans are **roasted**. Then, they are ground up. They become a mixture of cocoa and **cocoa butter**. This is used to make many kinds of chocolate. White chocolate is made from cocoa butter and sugar. Milk chocolate is made from cocoa butter, cocoa, milk, and sugar. Unsweetened chocolate is made when the cocoa butter turns hard.

CHOCOLATE, P. 2
LAB TIME

Candy factories work hard to make sure their candies taste good. They have many taste tests. Workers taste the candies. They check that the candies taste just right. Could you be a candy taster? Let's find out.

You will need: 3 chocolate chips (2 chips from the same brand and 1 chip from a different brand), a partner

---

Step 1: Close your eyes.

Step 2: Your partner will give you one chip at a time.

Step 3: Slowly taste the chip. Let it melt in your mouth. Write how the chip tastes.

Step 4: Then, try another chip. Do the same as you did in Step 3.

Step 5: Finally, try the last chip. Again, do the same as you did in Step 3. Can you tell which two chips are the same?

Step 6: Now, let your partner be the taster. Repeat steps 2 through 5. Can your partner tell which two chips are the same?

Step 7: When you finish, write six words that tell about the taste of chocolate.

CHOCOLATE, P. 3
PUT ON YOUR THINKING CAP

Math Path

What is the outside of a chocolate bar called? Solve these math problems to find the answer.

1. $4 + 3 =$ _____

2. $9 - 2 =$ _____

3. $8 - 5 =$ _____

4. $7 + 1 - 4 =$ _____

5. $10 - 2 - 3 =$ _____

Now, put your answers, in order, into a calculator. Do not use + or – when you enter the numbers. Then, turn your calculator upside down. You'll find the answer to the question!

Word Fun

Directions: Fill in the missing letters. Use the missing letters in the shapes to solve the riddle.

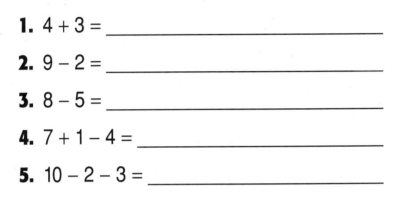

◯at   fis☐   b△rd   ⬭ouse   ◯ig

What are my favorite cookies?

Chocolate ◯ ☐ △ ⬭ ◯ **Cookies**

CHOCOLATE, P. 4
FIGURE IT OUT!

When things are heated, they can change shapes. Solids change to liquids. Liquids change to gas. Gas expands, or gets bigger. When heated, solid chocolate melts into a liquid. When boiled, water turns into a gas.

1. Water can evaporate, or turn into a gas. How would the glass look if the water in it turned into a gas? Draw a picture in the box.

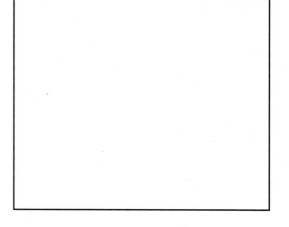

2. Balloons are filled with air. Air is a gas. How would the balloon look if the air in it were heated? Draw a picture in the box.

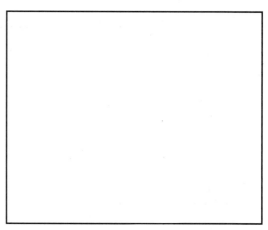

3. Ice melts when heated. What will happen to the ice cube if it is not put back in the freezer? Draw a picture in the box.

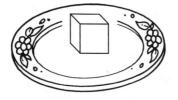

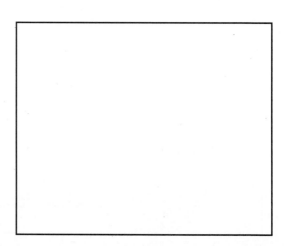

EX-STRAW-ORDINARY SCIENCE

Have you ever used a straw to **sip** a drink? You probably have. Did you know a drinking straw is just a small **hollow tube**?

Drinking straws were **invented** thousands of years ago. The first straws were made of glass. Paper straws were invented in the 1800s. Plastic straws were first made about 40 years ago.

How does a straw work? The air around you is always pushing down. It pushes down on you and everything around you. This pushing is called **air pressure**. Air pressure is always there, so you don't really feel it. Your body is used to it.

When you suck on a straw, you make a space inside your mouth. This space has less air pressure in it. The air pressure outside your mouth is still pushing on your juice with full **force**. It makes the juice go up the straw and into your mouth. Pretend that you took your drink to the Moon. You could suck on your straw and never get a drop of juice to go up! That's because the Moon has no air pressure.

REAL
FRUIT
JUICE

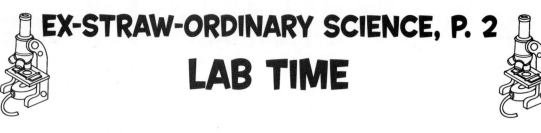

EX-STRAW-ORDINARY SCIENCE, P. 2
LAB TIME

Straws are useful for many things besides sipping drinks. Have you ever used a straw to blow bubbles or to make music? Do you think you can paint with a straw? Let's find out.

> **You will need:** cups, straws, watercolor or tempera paint, water, paper

Step 1: Mix the paint. Make your paint very watery. Use several colors of paint.

Step 2: Use one straw like an eyedropper. Put one end of the straw in a cup of paint. Then, put your finger over the other end.

Step 3: Put the straw full of paint over your paper. Drop the "blob" of paint on the paper.

Step 4: Repeat Steps 2 and 3 with other colors of paint.

Step 5: Use another straw to gently blow the colors all around your paper.

Is this an easy way to paint? How does your painting look? When it is dry, hang it up in the classroom.

EX-STRAW-ORDINARY SCIENCE, P. 3
PUT ON YOUR THINKING CAP

Math Path

Here's how to make your own measuring stick out of straws. You will need 10 straw pieces, each 10 cm long. You will also need some scissors, a pipe cleaner, some tape, and about 120 cm of yarn.

Tape the yarn to the side of the first straw piece. Then, use the pipe cleaner like a needle. Thread the yarn through the other straw pieces. When you are done, tape the rest of the yarn to the side of your last straw piece. Your measuring stick is finished. It will fold up and fit in your pocket.

Cut the straw pieces this long.

Directions: Use your pocket measuring stick to answer the questions.

1. Each straw piece is 10 centimeters long. How many centimeters long is your measuring stick? _____ cm

2. How many centimeters long is your desk? _____ cm

3. How many centimeters long is your shoe? _____ cm

4. How many centimeters tall are you? _____ cm

What else can you measure?

Writing About Science

Pretend that you are small enough to fit inside a straw. What would it be like to ride on a wave of juice in a straw? On another piece of paper, write a story about your trip through the straw.

EX-STRAW-ORDINARY SCIENCE, P. 4
FIGURE IT OUT!

Flying Straws

Did you know that straws can fly? Here's how to make a loop glider. You will need some straws, tape, scissors, and strips of paper.

First, make two loops of paper the same size. Tape one loop to each end of your straw. Launch your loop glider with the loops on top. Then, launch your loop glider with the loops on the bottom. Now, make a glider with a big loop and a small loop.

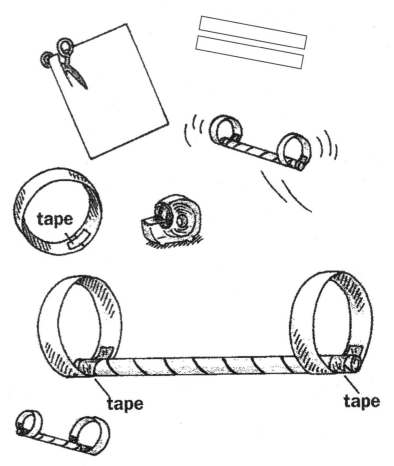

Which loop glider flew the farthest?

Straw Music

Straws can make music, too. Try this puzzling sound experiment. You will need a straw and some scissors. You should also have an adult to help you.

First, cut the sides off the end of a straw. Leave the tip flat. Bite down several times to flatten the cut end. Next, blow through the straw as if you are about to whistle. Do this until you can make a steady hum. Now, carefully cut little pieces off the end of your straw while you blow.

What happens to the sound?

BEST OF SCIENCE, VOLUME I, GRADE 2

ANSWER KEY

p. 4 Overall Assessment
1. C, 2. C, 3. B, 4. C, 5. B, 6. A, 7. B, 8. A

p. 5 Unit 1 Assessment
1. A, 2. A, 3. C, 4. B, 5. A, 6. B, 7. C, 8. C

p. 8
Lab: This is an example of sensory adaptation. The hand that has been in the cold water will feel the lukewarm water as warm or hot; the hand that has been in the hot water will perceive the lukewarm water as cool or cold.

p. 9
Answers will vary.

p. 10
Answers may vary; accept reasonable answers. 1. D, 2. E, 3. A, 4. C, 5. B

p. 12
The students should not see anything in the box when the lid is closed. When the lid is lifted, they should be able to see the crayon. They cannot see the crayon in the dark because for someone to see something, light must be shining on it.

p. 13
Science Words: 1. b, 2. d, 3. a, 4. c; Writing: Check students' lists.

p. 14
The lines are the same length. The black circles are the same size.

p. 16
Lab: The sound should be louder through the bag of air because sound travels better through air than through cotton, which is a sound deadener.

p. 17
Math: 1. 8, 2. 5, 3. 10; Vocabulary: Answers will vary. Some acceptable words are ear, he, hear, hearing, a, imp, impair, pair, paired, air, aired, red.

p. 21
Math: 1. 8, 2. 12, 3. orange, 4. orange; Words: 1. smell, 2. sneeze, 3. sniff, 4. stuffed

p. 22
1. digging up roots, 2. finding insects and worms, 3. hunting other animals.

p. 25
Some answers may vary. 1. cat, 2. rock, 3. alligator, 4. spoon

p. 28
Lab: List A was probably hardest to remember; it contains unfamiliar, scrambled words. List C was probably easiest to remember; it contains a full sentence, which is easiest to remember.

p. 29
Science Words: The six words in dark print are remember, important, facts, computers, store, recalls. Writing: Answers will vary.

p. 32
Lab: Students' charts should show more breaths during exercise.

p. 33
Math: 1. 2-year-old, 2. 8 hours, 3. 7-year-old

p. 34
Awake: 1, 8; Both: 2, 4; Asleep: 3, 5, 6, 7

p. 35 Unit 2 Assessment
1. A, 2. B, 3. A, 4. C, 5. B, 6. B, 7. C, 8. B

p. 38
Lab: When the warm air rises, it is cooled by the ice cubes. When the air is cooled, the water vapor in the air changes to tiny droplets of water. Then, a cloud forms when droplets of water float in the air. It is cold where clouds form because clouds are made from water vapor that is cooled to become water droplets.

p. 39
Science Words: 1. clouds, 2. water, 3. dark

p. 40
Top picture: Sun heats water and causes it to evaporate; Left picture: Evaporated water rises and makes clouds; Right picture: Clouds produce rain.

p. 42
Lab: Higher winds should cause more damage.

p. 43
Math: 1. 45 miles, 2. 20 miles per hour faster; Writing: Check students' lists.

p. 44
Check students' maps.

p. 46
Lab: The outward force from the swirling action will keep the water out of the center, and the water will begin to form a funnel. The outward force of a tornado's winds likewise forms a funnel shape.

p. 47
Science Words: funnel, lightning, storm, thunder

p. 48

Answers will vary. Check students' maps.

p. 50

Lab: If placed in a warm place, the seeds in water should sprout in 3 to 4 days. The seeds in acid should not sprout. Acid rain is harmful to plants.

p. 51

Writing: Sentences will vary.

p. 52

Students should circle trash on the ground near the picnic table and near the bottom of the picture. They should also circle the tire in the water.

p. 54

The water will evaporate from the celery through the leaves. The celery will become pliable and will bend. How fast the celery wilts will depend on the humidity of the air. If water is replaced after a short time, the celery will become crisp and straight again. As a result, the two celery stalks will not look the same after one is deprived of water and one has water. Usually after several days without water, the celery cannot be revived after the leaves dry out and crumble.

p. 55

Math: 1. soybeans, 2. $9.00, 3. $40.00, 4. $7.00, 5. $24.00

p. 56

1. clouds, 2. rain, 3. wind, 4. lightning, 5. snow, 6. sun

p. 59

1. shock, 2. crust, 3. plates

p. 60

1. core, 2. mantle, 3. crust

p. 63

Word Search: Check students' work.

p. 64

a volcano

p. 65 Unit 3 Assessment

1. C, 2. A, 3. B, 4. A, 5. B, 6. B, 7. A, 8. C

p. 68

Lab: The pennies in the pickle juice and vinegar should be shiny; the pennies in the water should not. The acid in the pickle juice and vinegar work to remove the oxidation, or dullness, from the pennies.

p. 69

Math: 1. 2, 2. 4, 3. 8, 4. 2, 5. 2

p. 70

Check students' drawings.

p. 72

Lab: Sugar is necessary for yeast to grow. Baking powder mixed with water makes a chemical reaction. Use a separate spoon for each bowl. Be careful that students do not mix ingredients from one bowl to another. The ingredients are not the same at the end.

p. 73

Time to Think: The recipes with sawdust and sand do not belong. Students' reasons will vary. Writing: Answers will vary.

p. 74

1. Students number from left to right 2, 1, 3; 2. Students should circle the right-hand picture, in which the jar is being heated.

p. 76

Lab: Plants should grow faster in the broken, loose soil. The loose soil allows the seeds to sprout and move toward the surface more easily.

p. 77

Math: 1. 3 ears, 2. 7 ears, 3. 10 ears; Pattern: Students should circle the far-right group.

p. 80

Lab: The popped popcorn should be bigger than the unpopped popcorn. Check students' measurements.

p. 81

Time to Think: Rosita has the white popcorn. Juan has the yellow popcorn. Eva has the hybrid popcorn.

p. 82

Correct order: 2, 6, 4, 8, 1, 7, 3, 5; Missing step: Turn off the heat.

p. 84

The two flowers in the sugary solutions should stay fresh the longest. The flower in the water only will appear less fresh than the flower in the sugar water and the flower in the soda. The sugar in the sugar water and soda serves as a preservative.

p. 85

1. c, 2. d, 3. b, 4. a

p. 86

The sugar in the warm water should dissolve faster.

p. 89

1. 7, 2. 7, 3. 3, 4. 4, 5. 5; word: shell. Science Words: missing letters: c, h, i, m, p; word: chimp; Chocolate Chimp Cookies

p. 90

1. Students draw an empty glass., 2. Students draw a bigger balloon., 3. Students draw a small amount of liquid on the plate.

p. 93

1. 100 cm, 2–4. Answers will vary.